FORCES
AND
MOTION

John Graham

KINGFISHER

This edition published 2013 by Kingfisher
an imprint of Macmillan Children's Books
a division of Macmillan Publishers Limited
20 New Wharf Road, London N1 9RR
Basingstoke and Oxford
Associated companies throughout the world
www.panmacmillan.com

Created for Kingfisher by The Book Makers Ltd
Illustrations: Peter Bull Art Studio

ISBN 978-0-7534-3367-6

Copyright © Macmillan Children's Books 2013

9 8 7 6 5 4 3 2 1
1TR/1212/UG/WKT/140MA

A CIP catalogue record for this book is available from the British Library.

Printed in China

Note to readers:
The website addresses listed in this book are correct at the time
of going to print. However, due to the ever-changing nature of
the internet, website addresses and content can change. Websites
can contain links that are unsuitable for children. The publisher
cannot be held responsible for changes in website addresses or
content, or for information obtained through a third party. We
strongly advise that internet searches be supervised by an adult.

Cover credits: tl Alamy/Paul Doyle; tc Shutterstock/Beth Van Trees; tr
Shutterstock/Catalin Petolea; bl Alamy/Janine Weidel; br Shutterstock/
Yuri Arcurs

Contents

Getting started

Have you ever wondered why things move the way they do? What makes them start moving? Why do things fall when you drop them? Why is swimming so much harder than walking? You will discover answers to these questions, and many others, in this book. It is packed full of experiments to try out at home or at school, which will help you to understand forces and motion.

Feel the force

Every time you ride a bike, turn a door handle or even just move your arm, you are using forces. They are the invisible pushes and pulls that make everything happen.

What you need

You can find most of the things you need for the activities in this book around your house or garage. If you do not happen to have exactly the item shown in the picture, you can probably use something similar that will do the same job. You may find that you can improve on some of the ideas here. Improvization is part of the fun of doing experiments!

Most of the activities use empty containers. Start saving plastic bottles, tubs and cartons. You never know what will come in handy!

Your experiments are more likely to be successful if you work carefully, and tidy up as you go along.

Having problems?

☹ If something doesn't work properly at first, don't give up.

☺ Look through the instructions and illustrations again to see if there's anything you've missed, then try again.

Athletes, dancers, racing drivers and builders all need to understand about forces. Every machine, from a playground see-saw to a space shuttle, relies on forces to work. From the tiny forces that hold atoms together, to the huge forces that keep the planets travelling around the Sun, forces really are everywhere!

Some of the activities need patience – glue takes time to set and adjustments may be needed to get something to work well. You don't have to do the experiments in order, although they make a little more sense if you do. The more you try out, the more you will discover about forces and motion, and the more fun you will have!

Stuck for words?

If you come across a word you don't know, or you just want to find out a bit more, look in the glossary or the websites section on pages 30 and 31.

Clock symbol

The clock symbol at the start of each experiment shows you approximately how many minutes the activity should take. All take between 5 and 30 minutes. If you are using glue, allow extra time for drying.

Warning

Read through all the steps for an activity before you start. Then work through them steadily – rushing or getting carried away could cause an accident. A pair of scissors or a hammer could cause serious injury.

Ask an adult for help. Take special care when using glue. Make sure you are using the right sort. Follow the instructions carefully and pay attention to any safety warnings. If in doubt, ask an adult. Have fun, but work safely!

Out of doors, stay away from traffic, open water, overhead power lines or other hazards. Make sure a responsible adult knows where you are and what you are doing.

Measuring forces

Forces are all around us. They are the pushes and pulls that affect an object's shape and movement. A force's strength is measured in newtons (N), named after the English scientist Sir Isaac Newton. On Earth, everything has weight. This is the force of gravity pulling things down. In real life, people weigh things using 'kilograms' (kg). But because weight is a force, it should be measured in newtons. So, a 100g mass weighs 1N, and a 1kg mass weighs 10N.

You will need:

- A large yoghurt pot or margarine tub
- String
- Two big paper clips
- A long, strong elastic (rubber) band
- Paper, marker pen and a ruler
- A few full food packets with their mass in grams on their labels
- A skewer

You will need:

- Two deep, empty cake tins, one smaller than the other
- A large spring from an old mattress or chair, or a large sponge
- A 1kg bag of sugar
- A washable marker pen

Make a weighing scale

Put the large spring or sponge into the big tin, then the smaller tin on top. Put the bag of sugar into the smaller tin. Mark the '10N' level on the smaller tin, to align with the rim of the bigger tin. Use other heavy things to make a scale. You could use kitchen scales to help you do this – remember 1kg weighs 10N.

What's going on?

In this experiment, the force of gravity is squashing a spring. The more mass something has, the more strongly gravity pulls it down and the more the spring gets squashed.

Make a force meter

It is easy to make a force meter, which you can use to measure the force of gravity.

1 Find a hook or peg somewhere, then attach a piece of paper to the wall underneath it. Loop the elastic band into a paper clip and hang the clip from the hook.

2 Open out the other paper clip to make a hook at one end and a pointer at the other. You may need some help and a pair of pliers.

What's going on?

Things have weight because gravity pulls on them. The stronger the pull of gravity on an object, the more it weighs. Weight is really the force of gravity acting on something. The weighing machine works because the heavier something is, the further it stretches the elastic band.

3 Make holes around the rim of the pot. Use string to make a handle. Hang the pot from the elastic band with the bent paper clip.

4 Put the packets in the pot one at a time, and mark the position of the pointer each time to make a scale. Keep your eye level with the pointer. Do not overload the pot, or you will snap the elastic band! To turn your scale into newtons, remember that 100g weighs 1N, so 250g weighs 2.5N, 500g weighs 5N, and so on.

7

Squeezing and twisting

Forces can make things change shape. Whenever something is bent, twisted, squashed or stretched, a force is acting on it. Springy or elastic materials try to go back to their original shape when the controlling force is removed. Thus they can store up energy and then release it to make things move. Wind-up toys and some watches work like this.

What's going on?

You store up energy, known as potential energy, when you twist the elastic band. When you stop, the band unwinds and the longer matchstick leg turns and pushes the reel. The energy in the band becomes movement energy.

Wind-up toy

This intriguing toy shows how the energy stored in a twisted elastic band can cause movement. Ask an adult to find and break off the heads of a couple of safety matches for you.

1 Cut a thin slice from the wick end of the candle. Make the hole in the middle of the slice (where the wick was) big enough for the elastic band to fit through. Cut a groove in one side.

2 Poke the elastic band through the hole. Put a headless matchstick through the loop and pull on the other end of the elastic band so the matchstick fits into the groove. Thread the long end of the elastic band through the reel.

3 Push half a matchstick through the loop of elastic band you have just pulled through. Stop it from turning, either with sticky tape or by wedging it with another half matchstick pushed into one of the holes in the reel.

- A cotton reel
- A small elastic band
- Headless safety matches
- Sticky tape
- A candle
- A knife
- A skewer

Spring launcher

Fix the stick to the edge of a table with a blob of modelling clay. Slide the spiral, and then the cotton reel, on to the stick. Press the reel down on the spiral and let go. How far does it fly? What happens if you give the reel more mass by sticking modelling clay to it?

4 Wind up your toy by holding the reel and turning the long matchstick round and round. Put it down on a flat surface and watch it crawl along!

You will need:

- A wire spiral from an old notebook
- A cotton reel
- A thin, straight stick or rod
- Modelling clay

What's going on?

The squashed spring pushes the reel, making it fly off the stick. The more mass the reel has, the greater the force required to make it fly the same distance.

Explaining gravity

Everything is attracted to everything else by the force of gravity. The attraction between everyday things is too weak to notice. We only feel gravity pulling things down towards the ground so strongly because the Earth has a lot of mass. The more mass something has, the stronger its gravitational pull. The Moon has less mass, so gravity is weaker there. Nobody is quite sure what causes gravity, but without it we would all go flying off into space!

You will need:

- Cardboard
- Two half circles of thin card
- A ruler and pencil
- Sticky tape
- Scissors

Anti-gravity

You would normally expect things to roll downhill. Or would you?

1 Cut two pieces of cardboard into the shape shown. Tape the shortest sides together. Position the two pieces as shown above.

2 Roll and stick the half circles to make two matching cones. Tape the open ends together, as shown in the picture above.

What's going on?

The cones are not really defying gravity. They are actually going downhill. Watch the middle part carefully. Try measuring the distance from the middle of the cones to the ground at each end of the hill.

Do heavy things fall faster than light ones?

Find something safe to stand on, from which to drop your pairs of objects (a chair will do). Put the trays on the floor, one on either side of you. Drop both things from the same height at exactly the same time. Listen for them hitting the trays. Which one lands first? Try repeating your experiment to see if you get the same result every time.

You will need:

- Pairs of things that are the same size and shape, for example: a marble and a ball bearing
- A dice and a sugar cube
- A golf ball and a ping-pong ball
- Two cake tin lids or baking trays

3 Put the cones at the bottom of the hill and watch them appear to defy gravity by rolling uphill!

What's going on?

Each pair should land together. Gravity makes them fall towards the Earth at the same rate, even though they weigh different amounts. This is hard to believe until you see it for yourself!

Balancing act

Something doesn't have to be moving to have a force acting on it. Gravity is pulling on you now, even if you are sitting still. So what makes things fall over? Every object has a centre of gravity. This is the balancing point where the whole weight of the object seems to act. It affects how stable the object is. Things with a low centre of gravity are very stable. Things with a high centre of gravity tend to tip over.

What's going on?

A lot of the parrot's mass is in its huge tail. This gives it a low centre of gravity (actually below its feet), so it is very stable and swings back upright eve... when it is pushed over a little. You can get the same result if you make the tail smaller, then tape a coin to each side of it to give it more mass.

The perching parrot

This parrot will stay on its perch, even when you try to tip it over!

1 Trace round the picture of the parrot.

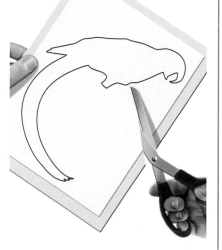

2 Transfer the outline to a piece of thick card and cut it out.

3 Colour in your parrot. Perch it on the edge of a table or on a taut piece of string.

You will need:

Thick card
Tracing paper
A pencil
Coins
Felt tip pens
Scissors
A table or some string

Magic box

Tape the weight into a corner of the box and put the lid on. Slide the box over the edge of a table until only the corner with the weight in it is on the table. The rest of the box seems to be held up by thin air! If you make a false bottom to hide the weight, you can even take the lid off to show that the box is 'empty'!

You will need:

● A small box
● A heavy weight, or several coins stuck together
● Sticky tape

What's going on?

A box is a regular shape, so you would expect its centre of gravity to be in the middle. Adding the weight moves the centre of gravity towards the corner. So long as the box's centre of gravity is above the table, the box will not fall off.

Under pressure

You can't push your thumb into a cork. But you can easily push a drawing pin into a cork using the same force. This is because the point of the drawing pin concentrates the force on to a tiny area, causing a lot of pressure. The pressure on your thumb is much lower, because the same force is spread out over the drawing pin's big, flat head. The more a force is spread out, the lower the pressure is.

Air pressure

The force of the air pressing on things is called air pressure. Although you can't see air pressure, you can see its effect with this quick experiment.

You will need:

● A plastic tumbler
● A sink
● A sheet of thin, stiff plastic or an unwanted postcard

1 Fill the tumbler right up to the brim with water and slide the card over the top.

2 Hold the card against the tumbler with one hand. Get hold of the tumbler with your other hand.

3 Holding the card in place, turn the tumbler upside down over the sink. Let go of the card. It should stay put, held up by nothing but air pressure!

Spread the force

Try pressing a coin into a lump of modelling clay with the flat side down. Then try pressing it in with the edge down. Which is easier?

You will need:

- A coin
- Modelling clay

What's going on?

The edge of the coin is much easier to push in. The smaller the area, the bigger the pressure of your hand's force. The coin's face has a much bigger area so it spreads the force, causing a lower pressure.

What's going on?

Air pressure pushes in all directions, including upwards. It is easily strong enough to hold up the weight of water in a tumbler. The card acts as a seal, keeping air out of the tumbler as you turn it upside down. In fact, air is pressing in on every square centimetre of your body with a force of about 10N, the same as the weight of a 1kg bag of sugar. You are not crushed because your body is pushing back with an equal, opposite force.

Floating and sinking

Whether something floats or sinks depends on its density. This is a way of measuring how heavy something is for its size. A steel cube, for instance, is a lot heavier than a cube of ice of the same size. The steel cube will sink in water, but the ice cube floats. We say that ice is less dense than water – in other words, a cube of ice weighs less than a cube of water the same size. So far so good, but how can a steel ship stay afloat?

Deep-sea diver

You can see how changing something's density makes it float or sink, by making this model of a diver.

I Cut out the shape of your diver from the pie tin. Make him tall and thin, about 7cm by 2cm, so he will fit through the neck of the bottle!

2 Bend the straw double, then cut it so you have a U-shaped piece about 2.5cm long. Slide the open ends of the straw on to the two ends of the paper clip.

3 Slide the paper clip and straw between the diver's legs and up on to his body. The straw should be on his back, bent at the top behind his head.

4 Make diving boots out of modelling clay and put them on his feet.

5 Try floating your diver in a bowl of water. Carefully adjust the amount of modelling clay on his boots until he just floats.

6 Fill the bottle with water and put the diver inside. Make sure the bottle is full to overflowing then screw the lid on tightly. The diver should float to the top.

You will need:

- A two-litre plastic drinks bottle (with lid)
- A bendy straw
- A large paper clip
- An aluminium pie tin
- Modelling clay
- Scissors
- A bowl of water

What's going on?

Squeezing the bottle pushes water into the straw; the straw's compressed air makes the diver heavier so he sinks. When you stop, the straw's air pressure expels the water and the diver is less dense, so he floats.

7 Squeeze the bottle. The diver will sink to the bottom. Let go, and he'll float up. With care, you can make him float as deep as you like!

How does a boat float?

Test your objects to see which ones float and which sink. Drop a ball of modelling clay into the water. Flatten it out and make it into a bowl shape. Will it float now? Try the same with aluminium foil.

You will need:

- Solid objects made out of different materials such as glass, metal, wood and plastic
- Modelling clay
- Aluminium foil
- A large bowl of water

What's going on?

Small, heavy things sink; large, light things float. But if you make a hollow bowl shape out of something small and heavy such as clay, most of the bowl is filled with air. The bowl and air are less dense than water, so the bowl floats.

17

Faster and faster

Forces can make things speed up, or accelerate. If the forces on something are balanced, it won't change speed. But if the force pushing an object on is greater than the force pushing it back, it will get faster and faster until the forces are in balance. Unbalanced forces can make things change speed or direction.

What's going on?

The boat is powered by energy stored in the elastic band when you wind it up. As the paddle turns it pushes against the water, unbalancing the forces on the bottle. It accelerates until the resistance of the water pushing back is equal to the force of the paddle pushing forwards and the forces are balanced. Then it carries on at a steady speed until the elastic band runs out of stored energy.

Paddle boat

This little paddle boat shows how unbalanced forces can push something forwards.

1 Cut four rectangles from the flat sides of the plastic container, 5cm by 8cm each.

You will need:

- A two-litre plastic drinks bottle
- Two sticks about 23cm long
- A plastic container with flat sides
- Scissors
- Waterproof tape
- An elastic band, about 9cm long

2 Fold the rectangles in half and stand them on their long sides. Bring the folded edges together and secure them with tape to make a paddle.

3 Tape the two sticks to opposite sides of the bottle about three-quarters of the way down, so they stick out by about 7cm.

Balloon boat

Soften the balloon by blowing it up a couple of times. Tape it to the straw and check that the seal is airtight. Make a small hole in one end of the tray, big enough for the straw to go through. Put the straw through the hole, blow up the balloon and seal the end of the straw with modelling clay. Put the boat in some water and snip off the modelling clay.

You will need:

- Plastic tray, the sort ready meals come in
- A bendy straw
- Modelling clay
- A balloon
- Sticky tape and scissors

What's going on?

The balloon pushes air out through the straw, which pushes the boat forwards. Jet engines and rockets work in just the same way, only they are pushed forwards by gases shooting out at the back.

4 Stretch the elastic band over the sticks. Use one that fits easily without being tightly stretched.

5 Slide the paddle inside the elastic band and wind it up. Put your boat in a bath or pool of water, and let go!

Measuring up

Measuring speed can be very useful. Car drivers, for example, need to know if they are keeping below the speed limit. Train drivers need to know if they are going at the right speed to get to the next station at the right time. To work out how fast something is going, you need to know two things – the distance it has travelled and the time it has taken to do it.

What's going on?

Average speed tells you how far the cyclist goes each second. For example, if the cyclist goes 20 metres in 5 seconds, her average speed is 20/5, which is 4 metres per second or 4m/s. Speed is often measured in kilometres per hour (km/h) or miles per hour (mph), but the idea is the same.

Speed trial

Here is an easy way to measure how fast a cyclist is going. Ask an adult to find you a safe, traffic-free cycle path for this experiment.

You will need:

- A bicycle
- A stopwatch, or watch with a second hand
- A measuring tape
- A calculator
- A friend

1 Measure the distance between two things along the side of the path (trees, for example). Try to choose things about 50m apart.

2 Take a long 'run-up' so that you are cycling at a steady speed when you pass the first post. Get your friend to time how long it takes you to travel from the first post to the second post.

Balloon rocket

Cut a few straws into 10cm lengths. Thread them on to the end of the string. Tie the string between two chairs about 10m apart; pull it tight. Blow up a balloon. Keeping the neck tightly pinched, ask your friend to tape it to the first piece of straw, and then let it go! With your watch, time how long the balloon takes to fly to the far end of the string. See which shaped balloons go fastest.

You will need:

- A pack of balloons
- Drinking straws
- Sticky tape
- A ball of string
- A measuring tape
- Stopwatch
- A friend

$$\text{Average speed} = \frac{\text{Distance travelled}}{\text{Time taken}}$$

3 Use this equation to work out how fast you were going. If you measure the distance in metres and time in seconds, the answer will be in metres per second, or m/s for short.

What's going on?

The deflating balloon squeezes the air inside, forcing it out of the end. This pushes the balloon forwards. Long, thin balloons fly faster than round ones because they are more streamlined and have to push less air out of the way as they go forwards.

Friction – the invisible force

Whenever things rub together, friction is produced. It is an invisible force that can stop movement. Friction also happens when something moves through a fluid, such as water, or air. Then it is often called 'drag'. Sometimes friction is useful when it provides grip or slows something down, but it can be a nuisance. On your bicycle, you oil moving parts such as the chain to reduce friction, but you would never put oil on the wheel rims where the brake pads rub!

You will need:

- A large wooden board
- A smooth plastic tray
- An assortment of flat-bottomed objects that won't break easily, for example a plastic cup, coin, rubber, or a matchbox

Slide or grip?

This quick experiment shows how the amount of friction between two surfaces depends on how rough or smooth they are.

1 Line up your objects along one end of the wooden board. Predict which one you think will slide most easily.

2 Slowly lift the end of the board and find out which thing slips most easily, and which is the most sticky.

3 Now try using the plastic tray. How much difference does it make?

What's going on?

Some things slide along the wooden board more easily than others because there is less friction between their bottom surface and the board. They will probably be the objects that feel smoother to the touch. Things slide much more easily along a smooth surface such as the plastic tray, for the same reason.

Rubbing hands

Rub the palms of your hands together, at first quite gently and slowly, then harder and more quickly. What do you notice? Make them wet and soapy, then try the same thing again.

You will need:

● Your hands!
● Soap and water

What's going on?

The harder you press your hands together and the faster you rub, the hotter they feel. This is because rubbing your hands produces friction, and friction causes heat. When you do the same thing with wet, soapy hands, the soapy water reduces the friction and so your hands feel less hot.

Force magnifiers

Levers and pulleys are 'force magnifiers'. How would you get the lid off a can of paint? You could use a screwdriver as a lever. Think about a door handle. You push the handle a long way to make the latch move only a little to open the door. These are 'force magnifiers'. A small force is used to move one end a long way, causing a big force to move something a short distance at the other end.

What's going on?

Because of the way the rope is threaded between the brooms, pulling the free end a long way with small force causes a huge force to tug the brooms closer together. The broom handles act like pulleys. The more times the rope loops back and forth, the greater the force-magnifying effect.

You will need:

- Two brooms or mops
- A few metres of rope
- Some talcum powder
- A few friends

Pulley power

Delight your friends and worry your enemies with this demonstration of your superhuman strength!

1 Tie the rope near the end of one broom.

2 Dust the two broom handles with talcum powder to reduce friction.

3 Get two or even four friends to hold the two brooms well apart from each other.

Levers

Ask an adult to bang the lid on to the tin really tightly. Try levering it off, first with the handle of a teaspoon then with the dessert spoon handle. Take care not to bend the spoons or make a mess! Which spoon works best?

What's going on?

The longer the lever, the greater the force. The spoon handle is the lever. When you press the spoon down, your hand moves a long way with a small force. The end of the handle pushes the lid up a little with a big force.

4 Thread the rope round the two brooms as shown. Grab hold of the free end of the rope.

Tell your friends to try and keep the brooms apart with all their strength while you effortlessly,

with your super powers, pull them together!

Gears – wheels with teeth

Gears are wheels with teeth round the outside. They can be connected directly together or joined by a chain. Depending on the sizes of the gear wheels, gears can be used as force magnifiers or movement magnifiers. They are used in all sorts of machines to change the speed or direction of movement. Bicycles and cars need gears to cope with going up and down hills and travelling at various different speeds.

What's going on?

A low gear works as a force magnifier. It is very slow on flat grour but good for climbing hills. The peda. go round quickly compared to the whee The high gear is for pedalling downhill or going fast on the level. The wheel goes round quickly compared to the pedals, but with much less power.

Bicycle gears

This experiment will show you the effect that gears have on a bicycle's movement.

You will need:

- A bicycle with gears
- A tape measure
- Some chalk
- A quiet, level path away from any traffic

1 Put the bicycle into its lowest gear.

2 Make a chalk mark on the path beside the back wheel, where it touches the ground.

3 Gently turn the pedals once, walking the bicycle forwards in a straight line.

Making gears

Mark the centre of each lid and ask an adult to punch a hole through. Glue a cotton reel on to each lid in line with the hole. Stretch a thick elastic band round the rim of each lid to give them grip. Push two nails through the card, spaced so that when you slot two lids over them their rims just touch. Turn the larger lid and see how the smaller lid moves. Try some different lid size combinations.

You will need:

- Jar lids of various sizes
- Wide elastic bands
- Thick card
- A hammer
- Two 4cm nails
- Cotton reels

What's going on?

This is just like the top gear on a bike, only without the chain to link the two wheels. Turning the large wheel slowly makes the small wheel spin quickly, in the opposite direction. To change into bottom gear, use the small wheel to turn the big one. The big wheel will turn slowly with some force.

Make a second mark next to the back wheel. Measure the distance between the marks.

4 Put the bicycle into top gear and repeat the experiment. How far does it go this time?

Circular motion

Anything spinning round has circular motion. Moving things will always go in a straight line unless there is a force tugging them off course. When something moves in a circle, it is constantly changing direction. For this to happen, there has to be a force pulling it towards the middle of the circle. This is centripetal force. You can easily feel this force on a playground roundabout, tugging on your arms as your body tries to fly off in a straight line!

What's going on?

As the cork spins faster, the centripetal force needed to keep it going round in a circle, instead of flying off in a straight line, increases. This force tugs on the string, lifting the weight up. The faster you spin the cork, the higher the weight is lifted until it reaches the cotton reel.

Spinning force

This experiment shows how centripetal force increases, the faster something spins round. Find a space away from anyone else to do this!

You will need:

- A cork or rubber bung
- About 1m of string
- A cotton reel
- A small weight, such as a wooden block
- A drill (ask an adult)

1 Ask an adult to drill a small hole lengthwise through the cork.

2 Thread one end of the string through the cork and tie a knot in the end, big enough to stop the cork sliding off.

3 Thread the other end of the string through the cotton reel and tie it to the weight.

Make a spinner

Draw a circle on the card and cut it out. Carefully push the pointed end of a pencil through the centre of the circle. Spin the pencil on a smooth, flat surface. What happens if the card is low down on the pencil?

You will need:

- A pair of compasses
- Card or thin, stiff plastic
- Scissors
- A pencil

What's going on?

Spinning objects, such as wheels, resist being tilted. This makes them stable. The spinner balances the pencil, especially when the centre of gravity is kept low by having the card low down on the pencil.

4 Hold the cotton reel. Start whirling the cork round in a circle, slowly at first and then faster and faster.

Glossary

ACCELERATION When an object increases its speed, it is accelerating. Acceleration is measured in metres per second squared (m/s^2).

AIR PRESSURE The pressure caused by the weight of the Earth's atmosphere, also called atmospheric pressure. Although it is invisible, air has mass, so it is pulled down by the Earth's gravity. The pressure of the air at the Earth's surface is about ten newtons per square centimetre (10N/cm^2). Weather maps show areas of higher or lower air pressure, as these have a strong effect on the weather.

BALANCED FORCES Forces that do not cause any change in the motion of an object, when they interact, are said to be balanced. When you sit on a chair, for example, the force of gravity pulling you down is balanced by the equal and opposite reaction force of the chair pushing you up.

CENTRE OF GRAVITY (or centre of mass) The point in an object where the force of gravity appears to act. If it is suspended from any point on the vertical line passing through its centre of gravity, the object will stay balanced.

CENTRIPETAL FORCE The force that causes something to move in a circular path. When you twirl a stone around on a string, you have to pull on the string to keep the stone from flying off in a straight line. The force of the string tugging on the stone is the centripetal force.

DENSITY How much mass something has in relation to its volume. Density is a substance's mass divided by its volume, measured in grams per centimetre cubed (g/cm^3).

DRAG An aerodynamic force that resists the forward motion of an object. The shape of the object affects the amount of drag.

ENERGY The ability to do work. Work is done whenever a force moves through a distance, so you can think of energy as a 'promise' to do work. There are several kinds of energy, such as light, heat, electrical energy and potential energy. Both work and energy are measured in joules (J).

FORCE MAGNIFIER A machine where a small force moving a long distance causes a big force to move a small distance – for example, a door handle opening a door.

FORCES The pushes or pulls that can change something's speed, shape or direction. Forces are measured in newtons (N).

FRICTION The rubbing force that resists movement when things slide against each other.

GEARS Toothed wheels used in machines to make one wheel turn another.

GRAVITATIONAL PULL The pull of one object on another due to the force of gravity. For example, the Earth's gravity keeps satellites travelling in orbit around the planet.

GRAVITY A force of attraction that pulls everything towards everything else.

The strength of attraction depends on the mass of the objects and how far apart they are.

INERTIA The tendency of any object to stay still or move steadily in a straight line unless a force makes it do otherwise. The more mass something has, the greater its inertia.

KILOGRAM (kg) The standard unit of mass. A volume of one litre of water has a mass of one kilogram.

LEVER A rigid bar that can turn on a pivot or hinge to transmit a force from one place to another. Wheelbarrows, scissors and the body's muscles and joints are all examples of lever systems.

MACHINE A device that does work. Machines are designed to make life easier for us.

MASS The amount of material that an object contains.

MOTION Motion occurs when something changes its position.

MOVEMENT MAGNIFIER A mechanism where a large force moving a short distance causes a small force to move a long distance – for example, the pedal that opens the lid of a bin.

NEWTON (N) Unit for measuring forces. The pull of Earth's gravity on a mass of 1kg is almost exactly 10N.

POTENTIAL ENERGY Stored energy. When you lift something or pull a spring, you give it potential energy.

PRESSURE How concentrated

or spread out a force is over a surface. Pressure is calculated by dividing the size of the force by the area it is acting on. It is measured in pascals (Pa) or newtons per square metre (N/m^2).

PULLEY A wheel with a grooved rim. Several can be used together to make it easier to lift a heavy load. This is an example of a force magnifier.

SPEED How fast something is going. Speed is calculated by dividing distance by time. Average speed is the total distance travelled on a journey divided by the total time taken.

STREAMLINED A shape that encounters less friction and reduces drag. A fish has a streamlined shape.

TURNING FORCE The strength of a turning effect. The longer a lever, the greater the turning force it can produce. Also called a 'moment'.

UNBALANCED FORCES Forces that cause a change in the motion or shape of an object, because the force acting in one direction is greater than the force acting in the opposite direction.

UPTHRUST The upward force that acts on an object when it is immersed in a fluid. The size of the force is the same as the weight of the fluid that makes way for the object.

WEIGHT A measurement of the force of gravity pulling on a mass on or near the surface of the planet.

Websites

If you have enjoyed this book, the websites below will give you even more information on forces and motion. Many of them have fun games to play that will help you to understand the difficult bits.

Forces:
- www.bbc.co.uk/schools/ks2bitesize/science/ physical_processes/forces_action/read1.shtml
- www.engineeringinteract.org
- http://primaryhomeworkhelp.co.uk/revision/Science/ physical.htm

Motion:
- www.physics4kids.com/files/motion_laws.html
- www.channel4learning.com/apps26/learning/ microsites/E/essentials/science/physical/friction_ bi.jsp

Index